I DREAMED
I WAS AN
AFTERTHOUGHT

FIRST POETS SERIES 25

ONTARIO ARTS COUNCIL
CONSEIL DES ARTS DE L'ONTARIO

an Ontario government agency
un organisme du gouvernement de l'Ontario

Canada Council   Conseil des arts
for the Arts   du Canada

Guernica Editions Inc. acknowledges the support of
the Canada Council for the Arts and the Ontario Arts Council.
The Ontario Arts Council is an agency of the Government of Ontario.

We acknowledge the financial support of the Government of Canada.

Allie Duff

I DREAMED
I WAS AN
AFTERTHOUGHT

GUERNICA
EDITIONS

TORONTO • CHICAGO
BUFFALO • LANCASTER (U.K.)
2024

Guernica Founder: Antonio D'Alfonso

Michael Mirolla, general editor
Elana Wolff, editor
Cover, interior design: Rafael Chimicatti

Guernica Editions Inc.
1241 Marble Rock Rd., Gananoque, ON K7G 2V4
2250 Military Road, Tonawanda, N.Y. 14150-6000 U.S.A.
www.guernicaeditions.com

Distributors:
Independent Publishers Group (IPG)
600 North Pulaski Road, Chicago IL 60624
University of Toronto Press Distribution (UTP)
5201 Dufferin Street, Toronto (ON), Canada M3H 5T8

First edition.
Printed in Canada.

Legal Deposit—First Quarter
Library of Congress Catalog Card Number: 2023951385
Library and Archives Canada Cataloguing in Publication
Title: I dreamed I was an afterthought / Allie Duff.
Names: Duff, Allie, author.
Series: First poets series (Toronto, Ont.) ; 25.
Description: Series statement: First poets series ; 25 | Poems.
Identifiers: Canadiana 20230580076 | ISBN 9781771838894 (softcover)
Subjects: LCGFT: Poetry.
Classification: LCC PS8607.U333 I22 2024 | DDC C811/.6—dc23

"You speak as if one's fate were a mere nothing, as if the mountains are inaccessible, and you insist that one can be content to gather a single strawberry in the lovely forest. Happy Creature, I prefer abundance. I need to disabuse you, for the clouds are not inaccessible and I have seen the mountain peaks and the ocean, its surface like a ripe fruit, with my own eyes."

— **Lucia Joyce** writing to a friend, August 8, 1932

CONTENTS

i.   A SCAVENGING

ii. POTION-MAKERS

A SCAVENGING

Some Disasters

What is the difference between *drowned*
and *lost at sea*?   Nothing, except

those who are lost might still come back, dragging
their satched spirits along fault lines

to visit the family home, or plot
to have a cup of Tetley — in a twinkling,

all was lost (the crash exceeded description) except
the bodies recovered from the bay,

heavy-lunged from inhalation
of foam, silt, and froth,   floating rumours

        of the unverifiable peace they felt underwater.

Oh, how lucky I am, I think, then knock on oak,
afraid to jinx what I've been handed

undeservedly; even superstition,
a kind of privilege, like taking

unnecessary risks just to find one another,
reaching out desperately, drunkenly, finally

barrelling down the Trans-Canada Highway
        in bad weather

or walking home along the frozen river, two loggers,
young men oblivious to the splinter

in the ice, a mouth
that will swallow then spit them out,

onto the shore, where they'll be found frozen
in the morning by their brother.

What is the difference?   Nothing, except a body
and a quiet place to rest.

Remembering MV Lyubov Orlova

Like a former socialite
she is lazy but photogenic,
sitting in our harbour for years,
        her ice-hardened bulk giving way
to salt and time,
becoming derelict.

No way to pay their debts,
those who thought to own her
revelled in her newfound uselessness

though she quickly became an attraction
for amateur photographers
and poets.   Maybe dereliction
was her way of making house.

Resisting those
who would tow her to be scrapped,
she came unmoored, drifted
into international waters

where her aimlessness
was said to threaten
the safety of offshore oil operations.

Now, she is believed to have sunk
but I like to think
she made herself scarce, stuck
somewhere between
becoming mythic
            (sightings
of her drift-born expedition
recorded like glimpses
of the unknown)

and, finally, dangerous.

The year the capelin refused to roll,

we still showed up, standing dumb
on the shore, strewn about
like seaweed under the setting sun.

In our hip-waders, rolled-up pants, and old T-shirts.
With our calluses, sunglasses,
and cigarettes

we waited, near-sighted, staring
at the fishless waves —

at all the nothing that can happen.

Like an indoor cat at its neutered window,
we focused just in case;
> but the capelin, easy prey,
> refused to roll.

So, with futile buckets in hand
we set bonfires like beacons,
blasted John Lennon from Bluetooth speakers,
and broke open another case of India —

later, we begged the ocean to relent,

to feed us once again.

Unlikely Sun

In late October
a brief heat wave descends
and we hurry to the beach
where picnickers dressed
in their finest Hawaiian
stretch out in lawn chairs,
attempting to tan.

We relax
but keep one eye on the horizon,
squinting into unlikely sun
after umpteen weeks of grey

and hold our car keys tight in hand,
ready to flee at the first sign
of atmospheric aggression.

For now, though,
the Atlantic takes a nap
from its ferocity,
breathes sleepy froth onto pebbles
where a stream, conscious of brevity,
gurgles slantwise into saltwater.

A trick
of the light; we blink
and it is winter.

The Harbour Mourns Fencelessness

How good to be swallowed up
to be let in
or let out

blue expanse
spreads

The Narrows —

a maw
stretching ship-wide

the fence stands
to guard the ocean from the town
(or maybe vice versa)

     I press my face
between cold bars
and will cargo ships

     to come crashing in.

The Icebergs Came Early This Year

In shipping lanes
more than 400 bergs wait

to jut their glacial butts
into the hull
of transnational
deadlines —

never mind
that the earth is boiling
(Would you like
a cup of tea?)

For us,
these pesky ship-sinkers
are harbingers
of a better-than-usual
tourist season.

Shortcuts

There's a cracked trail behind my cousin's house
that leads to the oldest church in the city

where in the parking lot
once
a man in a trench coat showed me
his pet mouse —

trembling grey thing
hidden
in deep pockets.

I was afraid then,
but not enough to run.

Newfoundland Summer

A photograph, taken seconds before
the eaves trough overflowed,

shows a thin strip of patio,

still dry,
protected briefly

from the rain

which rarely comes down so straight.

What are these strange
windless days? It feels
like I'm back
in Ontario.

#DarkNL2014

Something alive under the snow
makes it shiver
like it's asking not to be
shovelled, scraped, or salted.

For a few days
we get a taste
of living in the dark.

We get a taste
but are comfortable in the novelty
of seeing whole roads without electricity —

streetlights swing playground-wild
on their posts, taking a break
from the evening's usual illumination.

When some light returns,
NLPower begs us to conserve energy
and for once we listen,
understanding the word
when it rekindles our warmth;
we spread the message on Twitter,

every possible disaster
whittled down
to a hashtag.

My Nan,
forced to miss *General Hospital*
for the first time in twenty years,
naps instead, dreams
of Sonny Corinthos coming to Newfoundland
to meet her at Tim Hortons;
his iconic slicked-back hair
gets all ruffled,
messed and tangled
in the melodramatic wind.

Generalized Anxiety

I believe catastrophe
will send a warning letter, postmarked
for the next business day.

Tragedy will give advance notice
through portents: a gloomy cloud
or two above the house,
a crow with crooked feathers;
a black cat
pissing on the front lawn.

In reality,
when hurricanes plummet towards us,
I have time to prepare
thanks to the weather channel,
a barometric migraine,
and a concerned call
from my Nan.

The Snow Came Late This Year

Pop of pastel
dominates the driveway's edge.

Flowers are scarce
yet visible,

like little prophets
raising their pink hands
skyward.

Neighbours are grateful
for the iceless sidewalks,

except the not-so-scattered few
who believe in skis, shovels,

and snowblowers. Jagged mouths,
once loud with whir and spit

go quiet, worrying
maybe the snow won't come at all ...

Writing now, in January, I think
I'm jinxing it,   as they say:

If it goes out like a lamb, we'll follow suit.

An Onslaught

The blizzard won't quit
until we hunker,
bowing to the weight of ceiling-high snow
that entombs our door,

then caves inward,
collapses, melting in our hallway
like a drunken guest.

Days later, a moose is spotted
in the suburbs, wandering
from roof to roof
of our still-buried houses.
Fantastically crepuscular,
he watches the winter-weak sunset

while we shovel ourselves dizzy
and meet in the unploughed streets
to laugh about it all.

What They Carry

All day the sun burns burgundy
in skies made hazy
by distant forest fires.

Trees in western Labrador air
their grievances, blanketing
Wabush with ash:

geographic ember-dance
blurs property lines, prances
through summer homes,

mapping charred regions
where blackened trees
can lean.

They get smoked out,
evacuated in phases, carrying
love on their backs.

The blaze, it seems,
follows closely, tearing
through evergreens

for energy.

Now, they check in,
sit in the sanitary waiting room,
their sooty clothes infect the place

with camp-fire nostalgia, as they
wait urgently for news

of smoke-empty lungs.

Of No Returns

i.

In 1929
my great-grandmother's home
was devastated
by an unlikely tsunami, the water

rushed to meet her
where she was usually
limber.   Imagine

steering your vessel around the point of the channel
to see a ruralized Atlantis
risen again;
foundationless houses, stores, and barns
floating on the bay like antique bath toys.

ii.

Imagine casting a net
to find the water emptied
of trash.   It's almost impossible

to envision
letting the so-called wilderness back, voting

to unsettle slowly instead of spreading,
unchecked,
motivated to prosper or at least
to be provided

with necessities the rest of the stolen country
gets to feast upon;
     from rags to fishes,
     outport to (unfeasible) outport,
we find ourselves urbanized, finally

no rush, but

imagine going back
to find your hometown reclaimed
by spruce, river, and morning.
Horses from nearby farms
wander round the bend of the coast
to feed on overgrowth. Everything
succumbing to the seasons …

On faded maps
I pinpoint the jagged outline
of abandoned towns, their names erased
so nobody can decide
to return.

A Reclamation

The Narrows
is a dark space
      between two neurons

where water churns, struggles to make contact
with patient cliffs.

Murk-heavy; fleeting afternoons
become dusk. Black soil
surrounds my bed. I doze through
brain zaps, my limbs
like dendrites bend and buckle,

then wake to thunder —
the sound like a ship
crashing into the harbour's iron fence,

obliterating
itself and the synapse
that stands between our grey town
and the open.

Of Shortcuts

On Pleasant Street, a pretty tree.
On Pleasant Street I threw up
off the front porch before rejoining the party.

That Christmas I could only listen
to Japanese pop songs from the '70s.
It was predictable, I withdrew
from antidepressants, hiding
down a familiar hill, where,

in windows, I saw medieval murals
drawn by millennial artists. In others,

men rubbed their bellies
like cartoon chefs.
On street poles, endless posters
for missing cats.

This city is full of shortcuts,
but none of them take you
where you need to go.

Some Capital Blooms

Spring: lilacs, cherry blossoms, tulips —

scent overwhelms the idea of pollution;
      pale purple perfumes the main drag

until the first rain knocks pink to the ground,
into the petal-happy gutter.

A festival for the Dutch flowers;
regal, they pose for photographs —

get consistently sniffed.

Early summer: rose, rhododendrons

(cherry trees revert to standard green prickliness).

The tea bloom reminds me of a singer back home,
it's her favourite flower, but I can't remember
my lover's birthday ...

some smell like butter, ants in the folds.

July: lilies

closed-lip banana, pre-bloom.

I compliment strangers on their gardens …
They squint, suspicious:
Don't pick anything!

Constance Bay

High in the red oaks
blackbirds dive and land,
scattering clouds of white moths.

Sentenced to hunt
each moment and pin it down;
the past is mine, the past is mine,
and it's nobody's, too.

Neighbour's chainsaw
interrupts the call of the loon
(Or is it the other way around?)

The space between branches
is a green place
unconcerned
with my leaving.

Underbellies

Sometimes I mistake seagulls for meteorites.

Glowing specks briefly occupy
black gaps between clouds;

their underbellies reflect
the city lights at dusk.

Early in isolation
I find solace
on my paint-chipped deck.
I lie on my back, breathing,

and the birch tree makes a sound like breath, as well.

Motherly Instincts

Her nest another task on a to-do list,
she takes her time, doesn't mind
that a small crowd gathers to snap pictures
of her ritual.

Some concerned citizens call 311 and report
a snapping turtle
dangerously close to the bike path.

This tough-shelled lady gives no fucks;
she poses for photos without flinch,
her back legs paddling soil, persistent
as the river next door.

Soon she will abandon these responsibilities
for an unburdened evening.
The hole dug and covered,
she will forget these eggs

the moment she strolls away.

One Thing, Another

Her house is a postcard painted blue
that she sends from the Mesopelagic zone —

in the corner, a note: *There is just enough light here
to survive.*

Her open guitar case is a bed for the cat

whose own bed is a reminder
        of absence,

while her credit card
opens one door
just to close another.

If she must, she'll go
        to Rideau mall's rooftop garden,

full of rabbits
who get fuller by the trash-can minutes,

and have a cup of coffee, to go;
a comfort,   to pollute.

At the market, past midnight,
she carries a can of bear spray;

        if interrogated about her choice
of weapon, she'll say

there was once a bear at Byward,

on the loose, searching
for black spruce, and who's to assume

he won't be back again?

Before Last Call

As a teenager I loved wandering
alone at night, soaking in summer's silence
till dawn.
      Was there just as much danger then,
when I imagined myself camouflaged,

as here, now?
Where the life of the night
swoops in to steal my cab
but Uber, unstealable,
will get me home.

At a park in Hintonburg
the stoners and bats
make a display of chasing fireflies
who hide, briefly

elusive till they blink or whir:
They give themselves
away.

A chirp from my phone, almost
dead, reminds me to flee
from Elgin before last call;

before the spill, sidewalks that flood
with stumble, fight,
and a phantom kind
of flight.

For Those Unafraid to Trespass

On Canada Day I trip
over train tracks — patches
of grass exploding through rotten wood —
to claim a spot along the bridge
above the wide river.

I won't remember
who I was with, except
the bearded theatre actor
I met days before. He smokes
too many cigarettes and laments
the splintered side effects
of Thorazine and whiskey.

On Prince of Wales Bridge we watch fireworks
with mixed drinks and mixed feelings

while the geese and landwash
flow onward. All dampness,
teenagers in swim shorts
start fires that don't survive
past twig and ember —

down below, gulls on their mating rocks
make a racket to combat
the obnoxious things we do
to celebrate.

Retiree

You'll do better with someone
who can sit still, I say
on my last day at the office.

On Elgin Street, the squirrels
create a database for their acorns.

Meanwhile, my feet like dactyls
crave less stress; I walk
too many metres in high heels,
late for work again.

I joke that I'm retiring at the tender age
of twenty-seven;
say that I'm hibernating.

I say that I'm hibernating,
but can't relax
in my house with roommates buzzing.

In the hallway
my fern is in a perpetual state
of almost dying.

In a perpetual state
of almost surviving
I apply again
to work full-time.

Into the Hollow

Spring inverts expectations with something
pretty in the muck, bending its freckled neck
skyward.

With my best friend's golden dog
I walk on leftover snow,
standing tall for a moment
to correct bad posture

when suddenly thunder comes
like an alarm
above Alexandra Bridge,
and I tell the dog to run for it!

No longer nimble, we
slip on slopes and slush, gallop
knock-kneed to Sparks Street

where the boom of condos being born
blends with the wind.

The rain comes, finally,
and of all things
my period starts, too, leaks

down my leg
into the hollow behind my knee.

I've never been afraid
like this, of thunder,
but these are strange months.

At home in bed,
my body like a furled umbrella
curls into itself
as I sleep away
the stormy evening.

Stand-in

Already sick of the viral plot twist, the story written
        to make you gasp, instead

makes you hack and cough; in winter I travelled
        by train each morning to work.

Outside, construction was delayed,
buses ran late, almost empty;

        my co-workers, immunocompromised,
were forced into deeper isolation.

        Terrified, I moved back to Newfoundland,

and by luck became a stand-in on a TV show.
        On my first day they said

stand on your mark like a statue
        made of skin. Behind my mask I fretted.

Didn't we all? Lit up day-for-night, swallowing panic
        as we crowded onto set, grips

carrying ladders, apple boxes, rope ...
        I pulled down my mask

for a second, they needed to see my mouth;
        how the light played on my face. This wasn't

how I imagined myself
        reintroduced to heat, to breath,

after months of sweatless quarantine.

        Concerns
brushed aside as bodies brushed against me,

remembering the summer when I hid
        in a house too big for the three of us;

me, the girl, and the mother.
        Me, almost thirty; a live-in nanny.

Living rent-free for the first time in seven years
        an old tension lifted, like tugging down a mask
        to take a gulp of fresh air.

On the beach
the child and I learned the Spanish words
        for star, sand, and rolling, then forgot them

as we frolicked to see a watercolour scene: cottonweed
        spread on the air at sunset. And I forgot

for a second how much it costs to live
        and how much I'm afraid to keep going.

My grandfather likes St. John's, except for the

goddamn wind.
Everything gone sideways,
and I can relate. Bend into it, scalp first
like a bull in the ring;
it burns skin rosacea-red,
chafes like stubborn tuckamore.

Rattles glass in townhouses
that are dreamy upon viewing
but turn sinister, haunted by black mould,
after the lease is signed.

My grandfather asks me again
where I live. He forgets
each time I leave, his eyes
searching, clouded by cataracts.

These early signs.

Like sharpness in the air
on a sunny day — a reminder
that storms lay in wait,
ready to engulf
everything in grey.

The Labrador Current

Walking home after mass,
Nan wears a brown hat,
her head bent against the gale.

My friend and I trail behind,
flapping makeshift wings.
Our jackets, pulled
over our heads, like parachutes
drag us laughing backwards
down the winding street.

But this is only the beginning:
the Labrador current's baby-step breeze
before it stomps into blizzard season.

Nan calls for us
to hurry up home but a stray gust
catches in my coat
and next thing I'm flown three feet high,
carried for a moment, and I gasp
at how far I can get
before falling.

Annual General Meeting of the Tors Cove Sheep

By boatloads they were hemmed and jostled.
Hundreds of cuddle-faced ruminants
brought by Noah's hilarious dory
to their summer-long baycation.

Squint to see these white specks across the bay
on a green island-cliff; a flock
enjoying blueberry season.

At the annual general meeting
of the Tors Cove sheep,
shear-holders, regimented
and rosacea-cheeked,
are regarded with suspicion
but soon all are shorn and ready for heat.

They discuss leaves of absence,
the winter's woolly accomplishments,
and bleat their mission statement:
to cud chew for hours
on forbs, clover, and grass

indulgently, without
        dividends.

A Scavenging

Of shabbiness, they know plenty.
They lift off clumsily
from one trash-drunk corner of Robin Hood Bay
to scrounge on scraps
and preen knit-grey underclothes.

Scavengers, they hover in delight,
flap their saucy-winged surprise
as cars pull away, leaving unlicked foil
and cans that overflow.

After decorating windshields,
they crash a party at the lake
only to be chased, pushed aside.

Tuxedo ducks and wedding-white swans
are better prized by gloved hands that feed;
even pigeons are better dressed.

They scream their indignation,
but still get shoo'ed.

At dawn these gulls stand guard
on peaks, lining up roof-proud
to show off sharp curves,
hungry beaks.

Though feathered, they never quite ascend;
a photograph, instead, is taken of the clouds.

The Man Behind the Wheel

The monument at the top of the falls is for the fallen boy who jumped and drowned. We cannonball from the same spot, drift down closer to the ocean, cut our feet on shattered beer bottles — we don't notice the pickup truck parked by the cliff. The man behind the wheel asks us, *Have you ladies hiked this trail before?*

Later, deep in the woods, a man lurks behind spruce, one headphone dangling. We don't see him but we think we hear a gunshot (or was that a car backfiring?) over the noise of the river.

At the top of too many stairs, the wind picks up, stealing the breath straight from our mouths. The man, alone, talks to himself. We assume the worst: *He's following us!* Doubling back, we cut our own path through the brush — now, *we* pursue.

Following as he swears about money, gesticulates to a spot of moss, then spits. Back at the swimming hole, sticks and rocks in our hands, we see, from behind our thicket of trees, the predator-in-question splayed out across a footbridge, shirtless belly rising and falling in the heat. Sneaking off through the woods, we imagine a plot to kidnap us is still underway. Later, no one believes us when we tell them to take heed.

Drifting

"One of the basic situationist practices is the dérive, [literally: "drifting"], a technique of rapid passage through varied ambiences."
— Guy Debord, *Theory of the Dérive*

A Great Dane wanders Bonaventure Avenue. Bare-necked, gigantic, suspicious of well-trained pedestrians, he twists his misty nose in my direction. I follow the unlikely stray up and down, back and forth. Hopping fences on one of many lanes that zigzag behind Jellybean house and grey road, I alight on icy steps to smoke a cigarette, offer a puff to the wary dog who glances sidelong, sniffs a frost-dried flower instead.

When I walked here with my love, last fall, I casually mentioned commitment like a vine I could use to escape. He climbed down, away from the word, into silence. Now, a stranger crunches snow. Bolt-ready, the Great Dane keeps a healthy distance. *Is that your dog?* the stranger intrudes. *Sometimes*, I smirk back, and the man shakes his head, as if I'm just a child.

A Divorce

This island is hostile and I've been his lover
for twenty-seven years. He has a foot fetish,
so I hike twisted paths and sniff his ocean breath.

For months he takes the sun away, starves me, says, *Here,*
live off potatoes and beer.

When I decide to leave, he sends
fog, thick as wool, that curls along the highway,

blocking exits.

He sends moose,
dashing dumbly into headlights.

Finally he pleads,
presents gifts of beach glass,
clear skies, and low tide. Grinning: *There's no place like me,*

and I answer back,
bark at the wind: *I love myself?*
I'm convinced I won't get out.
But then, through that brief bright opening
in the grey,
I do.

Mainland

Saying goodbye to you
was saying goodbye to an island.

I know this because of the dreams —

in them I can't reach you.

I travel from spruce to birch
        to red maple, down tree-lined highway,
announcing

my arrival.

Like the ocean,
you are nowhere

to be found.

Resettled

Wearing our grandmother's
lipstick and costume jewellery

we clumsily trace
the perimeter
of her forgotten island;

rivers there
      are bent arthritic fingers,

every stream
      of thought

      a crooked progression.

In winter, we freeze,
show our gold-toothed grin

— a brave face
as the ice breaks.

POTION-MAKERS

Five Things

In my fifth-grade science class
there was a unit
called Flight; I was assigned
the ostrich.

My illness: not enough dopamine.

My Nan's illness: too much dopamine.

The Halloween
just after my mother's partial mastectomy
she dressed up as both
the bride and the groom
split down the middle.

Because my father is a hair stylist
who spoiled me,
I have no idea
how to do my own hair.

Elizabeth Avenue Ghost

For Sam

You spill all the stories you never got to tell
onto an average city road, where asphalt
glistens like gunwales in autumn's sharp light.

Walking, you are goofy; a klutz
out of water. Unfit
for fluorescent light, elevators,
and stale wooden desks.

You ride a blue blow-up raft
down Rennies River, dodging rocks and falls;
a pubescent pirate,
all bravado and noise, the other boys
egging you on, but it's shallow enough
in places that the raft sinks, scraping
the gravel bottom. Still I float, am moved

in the wake of this memory. Am I doomed
to retrace these moments of youth?
Haunting the park where you
almost kissed me,
where stretches of dew-soaked grass writhed
with nightcrawlers, and teenage restlessness
filled the air like steam.

You chose death. Hauled yourself out
of the current; soaked, heavy
from the weight of calendar days. I like to think

your last breath was a protest
against being gutted by the dull knife
that cuts us off from the place
we were promised in our early days.

to undo the curse I seem to have picked up
while travelling to Ottawa.
She brings me to her garden,
builds two scarecrows —
a mother and baby — out of branches,
a bucket, and a pink dress I used to own.

In Toronto, my mother is only fifty.
Soon, she'll need
Blepharoplasty; her right eyelid droops, affects her vision
      (the word calls to mind the sound I made
        when I vomited blood
        in Byward Market).
It's a minor surgery, I know;
she's been through much worse
and came out clear-eyed.

The child says the only cure
for my recent misfortune
is to prick my finger with a thorn
from the rosebush. *Make sure it bleeds*, she insists.

Over the phone, mom's boyfriend
asks if I have a birthmark on my butt. In his culture
it's a sign of bad luck — I laugh it off,

then rush to redden both my thumbs.

Nan Kept My Mother In

after one summer when mom went to camp, got stung
by a bee and nearly died.

Because of this
my mother encouraged me to explore.
Live fiercely, she said. *Get stung.*

English Degree

After too many grammar classes,
workshops, and open mics,
I became so afraid
of prepositions   that there was nothing holding me
together.

Re(wild) Children

That summer we learned all the secret words
for tomato, rhubarb, and squash. Words like
blush and bitterness; seed and impossibility.
Definitely invisible, we skipped through private property,
skirting the edges of fairy mounds and bumblebee
vapour trails.

      I had the panic-ridden eyes of a twitching
rabbit. A rollercoaster of uneven bangs.
She was sure-footed, surely trespassing. In the greenhouse
we were caught chipmunk-mouthed,
she, an expert
of deception, slyly performed innocence (winking),
as tomato juice spilled down her chin.

In winter we built a bridge — a crossing place, we decided,
for miniature moose, broken-legged frogs, and weary ghosts —
from a wooden pallet in the neighbour's field,
tinged with rot; age couldn't stop us.
It wasn't stealing; the pallet was abandoned.
We used old rope and badly-tied knots
and each day the chosen pallet progressed
slowly toward our freezing river.

Today, I'm uprooted. Unsettled. I'd give up the grail
for a taste of tomato, rhubarb, or squash.
I'm the spring-loaded foot following her
to dirt piles of development. Haunted mud
sucks boot from skin: delicious leather. Fearless

of rusty nails, sweat, and filth —
the squish of living earth — she walks
the rotted plank, and dives in.

Potion-makers

Under Grandmom's kitchen sink we find
ingredients hidden, we think,
for her witch's brew:

mason jars filled with bacon grease,
silt-like spices in clouded containers,
and chemicals, unmarked.

We make concoctions
that bubble unexpectedly:
        tabletop volcanoes,
        not quite magic.

We want
to inherit her power.

Instead, we're gifted brittle bones,
anaemic blood,
and just enough
of her iron will.

Nail Polish

Only the best brand names
for homemade manicures;
shades of pink with titles
like Flirty and Wild Rose

kept in the door of the fridge
next to the baking soda
and a glass bottle
of Coca-Cola,
half full — stored together in the cold.

When they grow brittle
from old age,
she persists, asks me to paint them
with shades of late August,
hues that drip like cool honey
from the brush
to pointed nails.

Aunt Joy, adopted,

is the odd one out in a community where most families,
afflicted with Catholicism, are a brood — homes bursting
at wooden seams with little ones. Food, scarce,

as patchwork towns struggle to recover
from the great wave, the War,
and the Depression;
men scrape together provisions,
poisoning themselves
in fluorspar mines
while women grind their knuckles, nails digging
into the month's ration of sourdough.

But for Joy, spoiled only child,
there is a whole red apple
waiting after Jiggs' dinner. Bullied
by jealous children,
she becomes obstinate.

They call her names, yank at her black hair
and poke at her eyes
to prove the point. If she could get bleach,
she would partake.
Instead, she insists that her hair is brown,
not black,
saves up coins to buy powder,
two shades too light,

and on the floor next to the bed
she has all to herself,
she kneels each lonely evening
to count her blessings.

Unconventional Oven

A wall mouse takes up residence
under the oven. I never see it
but I know it's there from the crumbs
it leaves — my Nan and I feeds it scraps,
hide a snack or two each day
till one day she finds it
dead in the corner of the warming drawer,
paws curled, reaching for alms —

we bury the body in an empty tobacco box
out in the yard, next to last year's cat, an improvised
pet cemetery.

For one whole summer I don't shampoo my hair.
I avoid the shower, white curtains pulled back
to reveal anxious thoughts, swirling steam.

When I'm seven
Nan shows me how to use the roller;
sticky scent on stained fingers.
Gently, we place newly-formed cigarettes
in a neat procession on the table.

A Diagnosis

With a lump in my throat
and clogged sinuses,
I hurry up the hill towards home,
sharp air sending blades
down my bundled chest.

All brawn and feathers
in my stuffed coat; burdened by winter
like a pigeon puffed against harshness.

At home, pamphlets on the lamplit table.
My mother on the couch, waiting
to give the news. For weeks

I'd had a bad feeling,
a nausea that spelled disaster
as accurately as migraines that pulse,
warning of low pressure systems;

pain, a barometer.

I phoned my father to check in,
sent a letter to my aunt,
and visited my Nan
next door. We built cigarettes

together, her tobacco-hued hands
skilfully sprinkling just enough
into the roller, while I held back
a panic attack
with deep breaths,
huffing the familiar smell
of her second-hand smoke.

Watching My Hair Dance in the Wind of the MRI Machine

Blue-gowned, lying face down
in a sterilized version
of a massage therapist's chair,
I hear the disembodied voice of the technician. He asks
how I'm doing, as the device comes to life.

I say I'm fine, but

I want to tell his voice that a loose strand of hair
is dancing below my face
to the beat of the weird techno beeps
the machine is making.

I want to tell him
I have monthly premonitions
that I'll die in a small space; some claustrophobic memory
haunts me, I guess —

> maybe the time my friend and I, nine and eight,
> had the brilliant idea to have a tea party
> on a hot summer day
> in the trunk of her car;
> we got trapped
> until her beagle heard our screams
> and started to bay,
> alerting her unworried parents
> to our peculiar plight.

Or maybe the time I got stuck in an elevator
in the Red Cross building
on the way up to find my mother;
only a few minutes by myself
in the windowless box, but long enough to panic —

instead I focus on my arms becoming ice blocks,
holding them statue-still.

The technician says they'll insert the dye now,
through an IV to search
for a spot of light that could spell trouble.
I get nauseous,
heat floods my groin, my belly; I expected
less queasiness after fasting all day.

Watching my hair dance in the wind of the MRI machine,
I think: *I'm only thirty.*
Then remember: *My mother was only thirty-seven.*
She survived because she was a nurse,
because she knew
when her surgery was postponed
she'd have to pull strings
to stitch herself to the living.

Then the machine makes a sound
like it's sending a guttural fax,
and I snap back to the present, remember
I forgot to pluck the sparse hairs
that populate my right nipple (but not my left)
and I think how desensitized the technician must be
to the varied imperfections of the body, how,
after I referred to my breasts as *boobies*
he almost repeated me,
an anatomical slip of the tongue before
correcting himself at the last second;
he blushed, and said *breasts,* instead.

The Last of My Lineage

i. An attempt to create a list of films in which a prominent female character does not want to have children.

Either they are superheroes (power, flight, flashy uniform;
stark contrast to apron-bound domestics) or they are
crime-fighters, like Jessica Jones,
except that's a TV show so it doesn't fit
the parameters. Remember, Black Widow declaims herself
monstrous because she was forcibly sterilized. Also recall:

> woman-character driven insane by inability to procreate.
> Unspeakable horror of barrenness
> pulls her toward the edge. Think
> of babies stolen from carriages by unstable heroines,
> unredeemable.

(When I think *barren* I see myself as a yellowed field.
But I do not want to grow carrots
from my belly button).

Childless women are seen at one or another brink. As in,
Thelma & Louise drive to the cliff.
Dani, blossoming in *Midsommar*, sets a fire.
And in *Melancholia*
a woman's inability to be a happy wife
is cataclysmic.

Then there are nymphomaniacs. Sometimes they are saved
by Christ or progeny: My pupils dilate
at the fun parts of the film
when they are allowed
to live freely.

ii. *The cult of perfect motherhood.*

Leaders monetize their Socials
with aplomb.
Soft babies of duck-print and yellow light
pose rosy-cheeked for endless photographs;

toothless smiles, puffy jackets, and pigtails …
She's a Cancer, can't you tell?

Think: Do nipples harden in expectation
of a mouth, of suckle, of feeding?
The opposite of erotic.
In a third-year sexual behaviour psychology class
at an underfunded university,
the almost-retired professor is adamant
that arousal during breastfeeding is evolutionary,

meant to strengthen the mother-child bond. *Yuck.*
Gross. Spit-up.

My own mother, unwed, milked herself
for my benefit, though back then
it was trendy to bottle feed.

I could never be so unselfish.

Olivia Colman delivers
the line perfectly: *I'm an unnatural mother,*
as she cradles a doll puking polluted sea water.

Then there's the guilt. Panic bears down on me
as if I've pushed a pram
into traffic,
my Nan's voice in my head:
You'll be the last of our lineage!

I internalize that time is not my own;
sell it, lend it, give it, sell it again. All these hours spent
writing, and I have to admit
that I'm still uneasy
about what to do next, or how to be
some other kind of woman.

After two years of waiting

it's hard to gauge
the significance of a month, a name, a palm
ready to grasp at straws to calm the storm
that gathers weekly. Meekly,

I tell the psychiatrist that yes, I can't stop spending,
and suitors are my only relief
from a looming obsession with death.

Concerned, the doc says maybe I'm
cyclothymic but that I should keep an eye
on myself; the system
is full, stuffed to the brim with everything but money.
There's no room to lock me in,
only drugs to swallow.

Like a squall that veers east
just before landfall,
I spin towards spring-coiled
thoughts.
I try
to pace myself
but sink;

I sniffle,
cough, and hack — the furnace, doc says, is ancient:
The air is bad, needs clearing.

Caught

Bare-assed, we sit on the hot radiator
to see who can last the longest, letting
red welts blossom on white bums.

We sneak
into our neighbours' garden,
learn to climb taller fences, scraping
knobby knees.

At 6 a.m. we toss a hundred
stuffed animals out the second-floor window;
a fluffy landing pad for our daredevil days.

Later, we lock the bedroom door
and pour a whole bottle of baby powder
onto the middle of the bed;
it mushroom-puffs, then gathers
in soft snowy layers on the white duvet:

Excitedly, we count *1, 2, 3!* and leap
on the mattress, sending
a frantic flurry that settles, hangs like fog
in the air. Out of breath,
we lie down, covered in talc and sweat ...

The front door slams
and we hear Grandmom's
scoff and huff —

panicked, we fan the powder
towards the window screen,
wipe it off the dresser, leaving streaks,
and sweep it under the bed
with guilty feet;

a futile attempt to hide
our childish antics.

God Bless

When I was young
we'd lie in bed, my Grandmom and I,
and count blessings like they were sheep;
she'd keep my child's mind relaxed
until sleep, counting
then sending blessings till
I'd run out of ideas, whispering:

God bless videogames,
god bless the neighbour's cat,
god bless the monsters under my bed,
god bless, god bless, god bless.

Back then I prayed for petty reasons
and lost my faith at seven, still
Grandmom was a fighter,
stubborn, our family trait.
She would not admit failure
and dragged my ass to mass
though I was an atheist at eight.

She leaned toward loneliness,
pushed people away
even as they tried to pull her close;
a tug of war of accusations,
she'd shout at my father,
How dare you have a baby at eighteen.
His answer:
You'd better not abandon me now!

Now, I'm left with little details:
The kitchen window in early November.
Leaves stuck to the pane
like soggy socks on summer-wet pavement.

I can hear the cat yowling
from the basement, waiting to be fed
and I can see dragonflies whizzing past the patio
where Grandmom hung clothes nervously,
frightened of bites from pretty insects.

For the last six years of her life, I confess
I never saw her, never spoke to her,
though I thought of her often.

I'll never know the truth of what caused such distance,
a continental shift between her and my father;
too young to recognize undiagnosed depression,
dementia … The last time I called
she barely whispered and I was sure
she hated me,
but I make no excuses;
I was afraid of seeing her in pain.

I never found the right words.
Not even now, when I beckon them.

I regret only knowing her when I was young,
knowing only what a child can know
of broken love;
confusion,
how the truth is a harsh sound
followed by a silent blessing.

I confess
the last time I saw her, pale on her deathbed,
all I could do was count the rosary beads
hanging from her frail neck
and whisper:

God bless,
god bless,
god bless.

I Prefer Abundance

Scoop a pint of cloud
into my open mouth. I prefer to be

the last one awake at the end
of this raucous apocalypse

on another Saturday night. And to sleep
for twelve hours straight, chasing down fragments
of dreams. Did you know

whole mountains
are born in ten-minute intervals
when I snooze

or choreograph, resolute? Sweat pours down the hours.

I prefer coffee medicine-dark, grimace-sipped,

and when no one joins me for a midnight march
into the waves
let them say I am mad or bad, longing for the moon

who does not ask permission to dash naked
from behind a little cloud.

Unbaptized

Underwater forests have imaginary names
uttered only by scientist, sea otter, and urchin. Still I find

something sacred every time I swim,
artifacts that sparkle when wet.
A paddling foot, tickled by kelp,

speck of beach glass nestled
in a patch of Atlantic-grey
sand. Sometimes I want to go back in time,

watch towering kelp
shrink to waving weed,
my own skin hauled into new light.

Born to leap
through fractured blue,

to hold my breath
and ask: *Did you wash your hands with brine
or holy water?*

Not that I wish I'd saved myself
for marriage, fickle symbiosis —

whole ecosystems gone awry,
disturbed by wool-dry hands, nets,
purple urchin overgrown …

Eventually, reasons underwhelm;
I ask then to be moved. I'm answered
by the tide.

Men I Have Known

M. gets a rush from entering
the forest. He lies on his stomach in the moss
and, bear-like, drinks
from a river.

> When I'm drunk,
> P. follows me home
> and tells me
> I'm too dramatic.

The next summer, J. asks me to help him shop
for better clothes;
I get cashmere ideas then
about what I mean to him.

X. finds me, no, comes to get me.
Sober wolf; drunk girl.
How do I say this? *I think it's my fault.*

F. insists that I smile.

> My freckles fade,
> sapped of colour by winter's gloom.

In February, K. is like a series of omens.
He's allergic to dogs, spiders, horror movies,
and honesty. He says cheating
is permissible,
as long as it's secret; if no one finds out,
no one gets hurt.

C. punches a hole in the wall
when I tell him how men treat me
but avoids the question:
Why do you think men kill women?

R. believes me
when I say it isn't my fault.

More importantly, I finally believe
it isn't my fault,
and never was.

On (twenty-one years of) Friendship

We're the ones who came to queerness late,
finding it with our fingers
like the first sign of laugh lines
at the ripe age of twenty-nine.

The ones who wear lipstick
under our masks like a fresh wound.
We burst into gas station bathrooms labelled
with the "wrong" gender, make patrons
stare as they pump and scratch
and squeeze ketchup onto blistered meat.

We're the ones who live with too many roommates
because Toronto;

who live with twenty-two many plants
because Toronto, again;

who were tomboys, weirdos, losers, depressed,
elated.

We're the ones screaming, *Is this the real life,
is this just fantasy?* at the funeral,
because that's what he wanted.

We're the ones who had too many sleepovers
to count, who walked to Jumbo Video every day
for free popcorn. Newly released,
the scent, inexplicably pleasurable,
of hard plastic and butter.

The ones who won the final game of spotlight
before the sun came up, changing the name
of the game;

the ones who have no children,
and have many children;

who wear winter boots at weddings
and leave the ceremony on a skidoo.

Who carry birthmarks and tattoos,
freckles and car accidents,
and went to the D.M.V.
on our sixteenth birthday
to pass the test.

The ones who say
we never lost our virginity, just
gained a sex life,
then twirl the duvet
around our finally happy bodies.

We're the ones who convince stubborn relatives
to compost and recycle,
the ones who haven't been back to visit
in years.

We're the ones who became teachers
whose students have it hard at home,
and wear their resilience like a familiar coat,
two sizes too heavy.

The ones who have a mattress on the floor
because we never saw the allure of adulting;
and who miss the comfort of the bed
shared with someone we called soulmate.

We march in protests
even though we fear
we'll trip over our despair.

We're the ones who type *on the bright side*
as our chapped lips silently mouth the words
I love you.

A Nude I Took and Never Sent to You

Like a ski slope in summer, I am green and out of order.

The mountains here are short 'n' scraggly;
on the bunny hill, I stumble.

Physiotherapist says it must be due
to weak glutes, hamstrings, but I know it's because
of too many grey days in a row.

> *I dreamed I was auditioning and had only silence.*

My friend is terrified of aging. Specifically of jowls,
so we do headstands daily, sticking our tongues out
at gravity.

> *I dreamed I was a squirrel and was finally prolific.*

I imagine myself
as a cult leader or a cephalopod;
it must be nice to have so many words,
so much nerve!

> *I'm trying not to be afraid of aging*
> *but the headstands do feel good.*

For company, I turn on
the fireplace channel and wait for the hand that stokes.

> *I dreamed I was an afterthought.*

We do headstands for so long
that our cheeks begin to sag backwards,
towards the sky. Great, I say, we've got reverse jowls.

I transform into an octopus
and give myself an eight-armed hug.
It's not porn if no one watches.

Our tits start tilting towards the sky, too,
and plastic surgeons contact us for an article titled:
"Best Friends Find Cure for Aging!"
You Won't Believe How They Did It!"

> I dreamed I was a ski slope in winter:
> Everybody wanted to go down on me.

We didn't tell them our real secret.
Instead we said we slept
upside down, hanging from our feet like vampires.

I'm trying not to be afraid. I'm trying not to be afraid.
I'm trying.

> I dreamed I was an afterthought, but I was smiling
> with my teeth.

Bleeding Through My Jeans at The Bonavista Foodland

In Newfoundland, April really is the cruellest.
From a TV production office in a coastal town, I stare
while the sun bursts through the clouds
for fifteen whole minutes.
I'm on my period and, painfully, the sky has been grey
for twenty-eight days.

Bored, I check Facebook, get bombarded
with photos of my ex and his new girlfriend.
Sort of looks like me, doesn't she?
She studied Law — fear of mediocrity
mixes with vanity's sting.
       A decade, erased:
       if I'm a cardboard cut-out,
       am I also the one holding the scissors?

My coworker tells me to use pain
as information; there's always more to learn
when it comes to loss.
Picking at my manicure
like an archaeologist of feminine beauty,
I scroll to a safer part of social media.

On the Bonavista community board,
an article about rare birds in Newfoundland
reads like a Christmas song:
Barnacle Geese in Bonavista,
Lapwings in the Goulds,
and a dozen Golden Plovers in Cape Race.

These lost birds, far from home, are called vagrants —
in the article,
an ornithologist named (I kid you not) David Bird
says that "Birds are like people. They really want
to go somewhere they're familiar with."

My film friends, flocking from big cities
to this bleak peninsula,
are like vagrants, too:
D.O.P in Bonavista,
Gaffers in the Goulds,
and Some Famous Guy directing in Cape Race …

Running an errand before the last location scout,
I feel my second-day-heavy period gush out of me
like a river tongue-kissing the ocean.
No time for the bathroom; the director is impatient
and they *need* bottles of water and snacks.

So I bleed through my jeans at the Bonavista Foodland.

The clerk helps me carry cases of water —
I wonder if he notices the cranberry patch
forming on my butt.
          After, I tell everyone in the office
that I have to drive home and change.
It feels like Junior High,
except instead of a sweater tied around my waist
it's a grey polyester blazer. Real professional
period-leak-chic.

(Just another ADHD day, carrying shame
for countless small mistakes but somehow, blissfully,
no shame for the blood).

Near the end of the film shoot
I can't stop playing Geo-Guesser.
Blurry Google Map cities
are claustrophobic; narrow streets
look exactly the same, but are thousands of miles apart.
Vanessa Carlton hurls a piano across the ocean (0 points).
I break my own heart, texting him again (-1000 points).

     That night I dream of shrieking into a pillow
     until my voice is raw.
     When someone walks in, catching me red-throated,
     I pretend I'm singing
     a gorgeous opera of grief.

The days get longer. My favourite time of year, usually.
Can't enjoy: it's freezing,
but the grass perks up, feeling green.

I numb myself, spend
$80 at the local consignment shop.
Red cashmere and striped designer jeans.
Buy a lotto ticket, too.
Bad habits;
sometimes I think he never believed
my diagnosis was real.

On the weekend, I walk around Old Day's Pond.
A seagull shudders
and the sound of its wet wings
is like a dishrag being shaken.
Crow lazily leaps from lawn to post, complaining
the whole way. Cocked head gives me a dirty look;
I interrupted snack-time.
These are no rare birds, but I ask
for their autograph anyway.

Driving back to the city, there's rain on the roof. Rain
on the highway.
Fog like smoke in the headlights.
More rain. I keep driving, waiting
for the sun to come back to me.

Here Is the Sound of Fire: It Is Smoke

Before the age of cancer my mother was never afraid
of bad styles or cuts: *Hair grows*, she told me,

but baldness has a way with words. On the highway
we hit a patch of black ice and roller-coaster spin
across lanes, onto razed land
where a forest fire shaved the trees
        down to blackened fuzz and stump.

Here is the sound of protection:
My mother flings her arm across
my seat-belted chest
and calms her breath to convince me
        we didn't almost die.

NOTES

Remembering MV Lyubov Orlova: Draws on information from the *Wikipedia* article titled *MV Lyubov Orlova.*

My grandfather likes St. John's, except for the: Tuckamore is a Newfoundland term for a kind of evergreen that grows low to the ground, bending to avoid the harsh coastal winds.

I Prefer Abundance: This poem was inspired by the life of Lucia Joyce, a dancer and writer. The *Paris Times* wrote of her: "Lucia Joyce is her father's daughter. She has James Joyce's enthusiasm, energy, and a not-yet-determined amount of his genius. When she reaches her full capacity for rhythmic dancing, James Joyce may yet be known as his daughter's father." After a long struggle with mental illness, Lucia was interned at St. Andrews psychiatric hospital in Northampton, where she spent the last forty years of her life.

The Last of My Lineage: "I'm an unnatural mother" is quoted from *The Lost Daughter,* a film based on the novel of the same name by Elena Ferrante. In the film, Olivia Colman's character struggles with feelings of remorse over how she raised her daughters, and with the regret of having children.

Bleeding Through My Jeans at The Bonavista Foodland: The quote in the poem is from an online CBC article titled, "It's been a remarkable week for rare birds in Newfoundland. Here's why."

ACKNOWLEDGEMENTS

Thanks to the editors and publishers of publications in which poems in this collection previously appeared, some in earlier renditions.

Bodies and Breath: "Resettled"
Canthius: "Nan Kept My Mother In"; "Potion-makers"
Contemporary Verse 2: "Five Things"
Montréal Serai: "#DarkNL2014"; "Stand-in"; "On (twenty-one years of) Friendship"
Newfoundland Quarterly: "Some Disasters"; "Annual General Meeting of the Tors Cove Sheep"
newpoetry.ca: "Seasonal Affect"
Prairie Fire: "Remembering MV Lyubov Orlova"
Riddle Fence: "The Icebergs Came Early This Year"; "Of No Returns"; "One Thing, Another"; "Drifting"

Thanks to my family, especially my parents and grand-parents. To past mentors: Agnes Walsh and Alison Pick for their invaluable advice. Thanks to friends, colleagues, and teachers: August Carrigan, Douglas Walbourne-Gough, Andy Woolridge, David Pitt, Tori Locke, Reuben Canning-Finkel (and parents), Gerard Collins, Kieran Walsh, The LSPU Hall (Resource Centre for the Arts), Spoken Word St. John's, St. John's Poetry Club, Heather Nolan, Rob Mc-Lennan, and Perfect Books Ottawa.

Thanks to Guernica Editions for taking a chance on my weird little poetry book: publishers Connie McParland and Michael Mirolla; associate publisher, Anna van Valkenburg;

cover and interior designer, Rafael Chimicatti; and to Elana Wolff, First Poets Series editor, for seeing something special in my work and helping me transform these poems into the best possible versions of themselves.

ABOUT THE AUTHOR

Allie Duff is a multidisciplinary artist from St. John's, Newfoundland and Labrador whose writing has been published in various Canadian literary magazines. She holds a Bachelor of Arts in English from Memorial University and a Post-Graduate Certificate in Creative Writing from Humber College. Poetry awards include an honourable mention in Contemporary Verse 2's 2019 Foster Poetry Prize (formerly the Young Buck Poetry Prize) and an honourable mention in Memorial University's 2016 Gregory J. Power Poetry Competition. With friends, she co-founded Spoken Word St. John's, a poetry open mic series that ran for eight years. Allie also performs stand-up comedy, plays music, and works in the St. John's film industry. *I Dreamed I Was an Afterthought* is her debut collection of poetry.

MIX
Paper
FSC® C100212

Printed by Imprimerie Gauvin
Gatineau, Québec